350

The Treasury of Clean
Sports Jokes

The Treasury of Clean Sports Jokes

Tal D. Bonham

BROADMAN PRESS
Nashvile, Tennessee

© Copyright 1986 • Broadman Press
All rights reserved
4257-18
ISBN Number: 0-8054-5718-6
Dewey Decimal Classification: 808.87
Subject heading: JOKES
Library of Congress Catalog Number: 85-27997
Printed in the United States of America

Library of Congress Cataloging-in-Publication Data

Bonham, Tal D., 1934-
    The treasury of clean sports jokes.

    1. Sports—Anecdotes, facetiae, satire, etc.
I. Title.
PN6231.S65B6   1986   818'.5402   85-27997
ISBN 0-8054-5718-6 (pbk.)

Dedication

To *Jerry Clower*
My Friend, Country Humorist, and
Sports Fan

Acknowledgments

Robert Larremore . . . Mr. and Mrs. Charles Tommey . . . the Tommey children—especially Sherri . . . you made it possible to put this little volume together. Without you, it could not have been.

A special word of thanks to my wife, Faye, and our four funny kids—Marilyn, Randy, Danny, and Tal David . . .

Contents

Introduction

Some of the finest humor comes from the field of sports. I remember Oklahoma University President George L. Cross saying with a grin, "We're trying to build a university our football team can be proud of." And who could forget Alabama Coach Bear Bryant's keen sense of humor when he quipped, "It's kind of hard to rally 'round a math class!"

And do you remember when Sam Snead was playing his third shot on the 16th at Firestone Country Club and asked the caddy which club to use?

Caddy: "Well, yesterday I caddied for Jay Hebert and he hit an eight iron."

Snead: (After his ball disappeared into a lake in front of the green) "Do you mean to tell me Hebert hit an eight iron?"

Caddy:	"Yes sir, he sure did."
Snead:	"Where'd he hit it?"
Caddy:	"Into the same lake!"

And what about the time "Dizzy" (Jerome) and "Daffy" (Paul) Dean were riding a train through a tunnel just as Daffy took a swig from a soft drink?

Daffy:	"Diz, you tried any of this stuff yet?"
Diz:	"Just fixin' to. Why?"
Daffy:	"Don't do it! I just took a drink and I went stone blind!"

Well, to be sure, some of the humor related to sports is often sexist, racist, dirty, and even sacrilegious. *But it doesn't have to be that way!* Here is a volume of sports jokes a minister can take to the pulpit, a Sunday school teacher can carry to class, and a kid can carry to school for his teacher to read to the whole class.

And as you laugh and laugh, be good sports about it.

TAL D. BONHAM

Ability

He threw himself on the floor and missed.

You know how much your father thought of your performance in the football game if he says, "Go upstairs to your room."
And your house doesn't have an upstairs.

Reporter: "Is there any truth to the rumor that football players are dumb?"
Professor: "A recent survey showed that 85 percent of our college football players are making straight A's, and they're doing quite well on the rest of the alphabet too."

Professor: "A fool can ask more questions than a wise man can answer."

Athlete: "No wonder so many of us flunk our exams."

A famous speaker once remarked, "An expert is an ordinary person away from home."

He continued, "An expert is: 'X'—unknown quantity—and 'spurt'—a little drip under great pressure."

Did you hear about the fullback who's been an undergraduate now for eleven years?

He can run and tackle like an All-American—but he can't pass.

A man was playing golf when his ball landed in a sand trap. Hidden from view, his repeated hacking finally enabled him to hit the ball out.

"How many strokes," asked his friends.

"Three."

"But we heard six strokes!"

"Three were echoes!"

A professor asked a star athlete how high he could count. The jock raised his hand and counted to five.

"Can't you count any higher than that?"

"Sure," he answered proudly as he raised his hand higher over his head and counted to five again.

One afternoon during practice a big, good-looking horse came up to a manager and asked, "Understand you need ball players? Can you use a .480 hitter?"

"You kiddin'?" snapped the manager. "Grab a stick."

The stallion trotted to the bat rack, picked up a bat, and walked to the plate. The manager served five pitches. Each one was slugged out of the ball park.

"You're a hitter," he conceded. "What else can you do?"

"I'm a great shortstop."

"Get out there and prove it."

The nag moved to short, and the manager started slapping ground balls at him. The animal fielded every one with tremendous grace and ease.

"Great!" exulted the manager. "Now go around the bases. I wanna see if you can run fast enough."

"Run?" neighed the horse. "If I could run, I wouldn't be here. I'd be in the Kentucky Derby."

Age

The aging catcher had a problem—he couldn't remember people. This became a handicap when he had to advise the pitcher what to throw to a batter. But he didn't merely fail to recognize the enemy; he didn't even know the names of his teammates.

When his roommate from the previous year met him at spring training camp, the roomie chided him. "I bet you don't remember me," he challenged.

"Of course I do, you're number 4."

Old age is when the grandkids come home and tell you what they're studying about in history—and you remember studying those things in current-events classes.

A baseball pro took over the management of a farm team after his tremendous speed began to wane. But every so often he put himself into the game as a pinch-hitter when a critical situation arose, and his keen batting eye could be of use to his team.

One night, this manager had a serious dispute on the field with one of the umpires. The patient umpire spoke few words despite the abuse showered on him.

Some weeks later the manager's team was behind by ten runs. With two men on and one out, the manager decided to put himself in as a pinch hitter.

As the manager moved to the plate swinging his bat, the umpire called out to the fans: "The manager now batting for exercise!"

"You're looking well," said a friend to a ninety-five-year-old former athlete.

"It's not my appearance that bothers me, these days, but my disappearance!" he answered.

One has reached the golden age when he becomes exhausted simply by wrestling with his conscience.

A Golf Ball: A round object struck by a golf club, the golf ball is 1.68 inches in diameter, weighs 1.62 ounces and costs about $1.50. By the time you're rich enough to lose one without crying, you're too old to hit it that far!

When the athlete who was filling out the application came to the little square marked "Age," he did not hesitate. He simply wrote: "Nuclear."

An elderly athlete neared his ninetieth birthday, and the local paper sent a reporter to interview him.

"Tell me, sir," the newsman questioned, "what exercise do you do to keep fit?"

"My boy," replied the oldster, "when you're pushing ninety that's the only exercise you need."

Football players on television wear a lot of tape these days.

After watching a football game on television, one elderly lady commented, "These players can't be too old. Some of them haven't been unwrapped yet."

Retirement: When the whole point of your day is to get the figure on your golf score as low as the one on your Social Security check.

Dad: "Is there anything worse than being old and bent?"

Collegiate Son: "Yes, being young and broke."

A reporter, interviewing a one-time athlete on his ninety-ninth birthday, commented, "I certainly hope I can come back next year and see you reach the century mark."

"Can't see why not, young feller," the old-timer replied, "you look healthy enough to me."

Life is like a taxi—the meter keeps going whether you are getting somewhere or just standing still.

Baseball

Late in the baseball season, a pastor was explaining to an elderly lady that the major league teams would soon be starting their campaign to decide who was world champion.

"My goodness," she exclaimed, "I thought they settled that last year!"

Sunday School Teacher: "Who whipped the Philistines?"

Student: "If they don't play the Reds, I don't keep track of 'em."

Husband to sniffling wife: "You and your soap operas! Why do you cry over the make-believe troubles of people you never met?"

Wife: "For the same reason that you holler and scream when a man you don't know hits a home run!"

Miss Smith stood behind her desk in astonishment. She had asked the class, "Can anyone tell me where Cincinnati is?" George, the dullest boy in the class, had raised his hand.

Nodding to the boy she said, "All right, George, you may answer."

"Cincinnati," chirped the boy, "is playing in New York."

A high school student decided to try out for his school baseball team. He arrived at the practice field carrying his glove and spikes.

The coach approached him and asked, "Okay. Name your best playin' position!"

"Sorta stooped over like this," answered the student.

Wanting to demonstrate his hitting prowess, a little boy was showing off to his father. Three times he tossed the ball into the air, swung at it, and missed all three times. At the third strike, he yelled, "Boy, what a pitcher I am!"

Fan: "Where did you put the matador who joined the baseball team?"

Manager: "In the bullpen."

Question: What do you get if you cross a lizard with a baseball player?

Answer: An outfielder who catches flies on his tongue and eats them.

The outfielder made a tremendous try for a ball hit down the right-field line but, instead of catching it, slipped and fell—and was sitting on the ball without being aware of that fact.

The manager stood up in the dugout and screamed out, "Somebody tell that guy to get off the ball before it hatches!"

A baseball player, when popping the question, put it this way: "How would you like to sign up with me for a life game?"

The girl responded, "All right, but where is your diamond?"

As a shortstop, he had one weakness—the balls batted at him.

A baseball celebrity began his ball playing in his backwoods community as a young boy.

One Sunday, the boy was on his way to the ball field when he was stopped by the minister of his church, who boomed, "Look here, my son, don't you know it's sinful to work on the Lord's Day?"

"Shucks, Reverend," smiled the boy. "You don't mind working on Sunday, do you?"

"Of course not," snapped the pastor, "but when I work on Sunday, I'm in the right field."

"Well, Reverend," said the surprised boy, "that's just where they put me—can you tell me how to play out there?"

Basketball

One government official in Texas had the ingenious idea of using oil rigs as jails for convicted basketball players.

A pilot was flying a group of basketball players back home after a game. When they were about to land, they were told that the fog was too dense to land right at the moment, and to circle till they could.

This continued about two hours. Finally, over the speakers came the voice of the pilot: "I've got some good news and some bad news. The bad news is we are about out of gas. The good news is I'm parachuting down to get some."

Motto posted over the basketball coach's desk: "Use your head. It's the little things that count."

A well-known basketball player complained to a reporter that he was fed up with all the foolish stuff they were writing about him.

"I'm no clown!" insisted the basketball player.

"I'm a serious guy. I read books. I wish you'd say something serious about me sometime."

"All right," said the newspaperman. "What do you think of the Civil War?"

A blank look spread over the athlete's face. He scratched his head for a moment and then drawled, without a trace of a smile, "I think it shoulda been scored a hit."

Boats

"I should never have worn my golf shoes in a rubber raft," the man moaned *deflatedly.*

Young wife to oarsman after his crew had lost the race: "Never mind, dear. You were wonderful. You rowed faster than anyone in the boat!"

The boat show had a yacht to offer. Phew!

Question: "How do you crash a houseboat party?"
Answer: "You just barge in!"

It now costs more than forty cents a mile to run the average American car while pulling a boat.

However, if you run it past a red light, it will cost you slightly more.

Bowling

Bowling: Marbles for grown-ups.

"I like bowling. I'd rather bowl than eat."
"Doesn't your wife object?"
"No, she'd rather play golf than cook."

A bowler remarked to the others when leaving, "Well, anyway, we didn't lose any of the balls."

A bowling fanatic played every Thursday evening. One Thursday he left the house and did not return.

Exactly five years later to the day, he returned home, and his overjoyed wife started telephoning all their friends.

"What are you doing?" he asked.

"I'm going to throw a homecoming party for you!" replied his wife.

"Oh, no, you won't!" he objected. "Not on my bowling night!"

Bowling: A sport that, unlike golf, allows you to start and finish with the same ball.

There Marie was, bowling first with her right hand and then with her left.

"Miss," suggested the alley manager, "you'll improve your average if you just concentrate on one hand."

"Oh," replied Marie, "I'm worried about my weight. I want to take some off this side and some off that side."

Boxing

The minister was visiting the homes of his parishioners, and in one he asked a good many questions about the family. A grubby, but cheerful, little boy attracted the kindly cleric's attention. He asked him his name, and the lad replied, "Bolivar Reginald Shagnasty, the Third, Sir."

The minister turned to the boy's father and asked, "What made you give the boy a name like that?"

"'Cause I want 'em to be a professional boxer," returned the parent, "an wif a name like that, he'll git plenty of practice at school."

As the bell rang for the first round, the prizefighter made the sign of the cross before advancing to the center of the ring. A fellow in the audience turned to the priest sitting next to him.

"Father, will that help him win the fight?"

"Yes," advised the priest, "if he is in condition and knows how to fight."

A fighter was taking a terrific beating in the ring. When he stumbled back to his corner at the end of a round, his manager looked at him and instructed, "Let him hit you with his right for awhile. Your face is crooked."

In a heavyweight boxing match, the two fighters circled the ring, striking out at each other in light and tentative fashion but never landing a blow, while making fierce faces at each other and grunting as though striving desperately. This went on for several dreary rounds when a voice from the gallery called out, "Come on, hit him, ya bum! Ya got the wind with you!"

A boxer was knocked flat in the first round of his bout. The referee began to count over the downed fellow. The weary fighter seemed to be conscious, but made no move to get to his feet. As the count approached the fateful ten, he rolled over and spoke: "Mr. Referee, you're very fair, but I just want to make it clear—I'm through for the night!"

The prize fighter wasn't having any luck in fending off his opponent. In fact, he looked pretty sick of the whole affair.

"Stop those punches!" roared his excited manager from the corner.

The fighter managed to move his battered lips enough to retort: "You don't see any of 'em getting past me, do you?"

Cheerleaders

A cheerleader told her friend, "I'm knitting something to make the boys happy."

Her friend asked, "Oh, a sweater for a player?"

The cheerleader replied, "No, a bathing suit for me!"

Why do some universities have artificial turf on the football field instead of regular grass?

To keep the cheerleaders from grazing.

A football player wanted to buy a parrot for one of the cheerleaders. He saw exactly what he wanted at an auction sale.

The bidding picked up fast and furiously! He thought he would never buy that parrot—$5—$20—$30—$40—$100—$200—$700!

On the way home with his parrot and cage sitting on the front seat, he said, "Now talk to me, you stupid bird!" The bird spoke not a word.

"Do you mean to say I paid $700 for a stupid parrot and it can't even talk?"

"Can't talk?" exclaimed the parrot. "Who do you think you were bidding against?"

Two cheerleaders were shopping for a team mascot in a local pet shop.

"Show us the way to the Labradors," they said to the janitor.

"Yes, ladies! The men's room is in the basement, and the ladies' room is down the hall."

Climbing

Never measure the mountain until you have reached the top; then you will see how low it is.

"When my husband first looked down into the Grand Canyon his face dropped about a mile!" reported a mountain climber's wife.

"You mean to say he was disappointed in the Grand Canyon?"

"No, not at all. I mean he fell over the rim!"

Coaching

Patience in coaching may often be the inability to make a decision.

Coaches may understand sports, but do not necessarily understand choral music. One coach had a gorgeous wife who joined the church choir.

"How you doin' in the choir?" he asked his wife.

"All right, I guess," she answered modestly. "I sing second soprano."

"Second! That ain't good enough. I'll send that choir director a couple of complimentary tickets to our next game. Then maybe he'll make you first soprano!"

Coach: "Now, if I were to take a hammer and smash this clock, could I be arrested for killing time?"

Athlete: "No, it would be self-defense."

Coach: "Why?"

Athlete: "Because the clock struck first!"

Descriptions of a few (thankfully) coaches: "Some

people have a chip on their shoulders; he has a whole lumberyard."

"Lots of people look up to him. That's because he just knocked them down."

"Run a team? He couldn't run a tollbooth."

During spring training the team was performing badly at bat. Finally the manager became so mad he picked up a bat and said, "I'm gonna show you guys something."

The manager missed the ball pitch after pitch. When the pitcher began to get weary—and the manager remained hitless—he threw the bat aside and yelled, "Now, you see what I mean? That's what you've been doing. Now come out of it and connect with the ball."

When a losing coach of a pro football team quit to coach at a university, he was asked what his new strategy would be.

"Next year," he allowed, "we'll be passing a lot—hopefully to our own people."

A fastball hitter was at bat with runners on first and third. The coach gave the sign for a double steal. So, after the pitch, the catcher threw to second while the runner on third went for home plate. The shortstop cut the ball off, then threw home for what should have been a close play at the plate.

When the throw came across the plate, the fastball hitter swung and connected with the ball. The umpire stopped the game and asked, "Why in the world did you hit that ball?"

The fastball hitter replied, "That's the only fastball I've seen all season!"

A coach quarreled with the umpire on every call he made, until a foul ball was hit into the stands, immediately after which a woman was carried out on a stretcher. The umpire asked the coach if the ball had hit the woman.

"No," replied the coach, "you called that one right, and she fainted."

The comment of a coach after a bad workout: "I wouldn't let my mother-in-law run behind that line."

The wife of a wealthy coach loved birds. On their twenty-fifth anniversary, he purchased her a beautiful mynah that spoke twenty-five languages.

He paid $1,000 per language for the bird. He sent it to her while on a recruiting trip.

Two days later he called and asked, "What did you think of the wonderful bird I sent you?"

"It was absolutely elegant," answered his wife.

"Where is the bird right now?" asked the husband.

"He's in the oven!" said his wife.

"Why, darling, that bird could speak twenty-five languages."

"Then why didn't he say something!"

An optimistic coach talking to the team before a game, "We are unbeaten, unscored on, untied—and getting ready for our first game!"

A coach, discussing the curfew and other rules concerning off-practice hours, opined, "Boys, you can't fly with the owls at night and keep up with the eagles in the daytime!"

A writer commenting on a coach said, "Human intelligence is thousands of years old, but it doesn't seem to act its age."

Conceit

"If I could buy a conceited person at my price and sell him at his own, I'd make a very good profit."

The game ended with the home team losing by 84 points. The school president asked the coach for a comment.

"It was a team effort," he replied.

Wondering about a popular athlete, one fellow mentioned to his friend, "I hear that he's changing his faith."

The friend replied, "You mean he no longer believes he's a deity?"

A famous ball player remarked, "I often quote myself. It adds spice to the conversation."

At the annual coaches' dinner, a sports writer spotted a coach who hadn't had a winning season in eight years.

"According to the preseason dope," said the

writer, "your team should win your division this year."

"Now, hold on," growled the coach. "What is the name of that preseason dope?"

A man who's wrapped up in himself makes a mighty small parcel.

The rookie pitcher, appearing in his first major league game, faced the initial batter confidently. He went into a windup and threw his pitch. To his amazement, the batter hit it—out of the park. The rookie glared as the batter trotted around the bases.

"You were lucky," he shouted bitterly, "You've spoiled my no-hitter!"

The secret of polite conversation is never to open your mouth unless you have nothing to say.

Critics

A sports writer reflected on a team's trading of players by writing, "It's better to tighten your belt than to lose your pants."

Critic: One who is quick on the flaw.

A winning football coach became enraged at a referee whom he thought had made a number of bad calls during a game. The coach yelled at him, "You stink!"

The referee picked up the football, marked off another penalty of ten yards, turned toward his abuser, and yelled, "How do I smell from here?"

A football team was having such a bad season a sports writer wrote: "The opposing team scored two touchdowns during halftime."

A big college football team had a record number of fumbles during the first three quarters of the game. The team's coach ordered a substitute back to warm up. During the warm-up the substitute dropped a ball that was tossed to him.

"Send him in, Coach, he's ready," called a man in the stands.

A coach of a pro football team had spent a good part of the game needling one of the referees from the sidelines. But he picked the wrong man, as he discovered late in the game when he was caught illegally shouting instructions to his players.

The needled referee called time, paced off ten yards, and said to the coach, "That's for coaching from the sidelines."

"That proves you don't know the rules," shouted the coach. "The penalty for illegal coaching is more than ten yards!"

"I know," said the referee. "But your kind of coaching is not good enough for the full penalty!"

Constructive criticism: Advice you give another player—whether he wants to hear it or not.

A college grad watched his alma mater play a football game. On his way out of the stadium after his team was badly beaten, the coach was stopped by the grad.

"What is the enrollment in our university?" he asked the coach.

"About 10,000," replied the coach.

"Well, why can't you get a few of them and put them in front of the man who is carrying the ball?" asked the grad.

An Englishman told an American hunter that he had shot thirty-three hares before breakfast.

"Thirty-three hairs!" exclaimed the American. "You musta been firing at a wig."

Cycling

First Law of Bicycling—No matter which way you ride, it's uphill and against the wind.

An officer stopped a man and his wife on their motorcycle and suggested they visit the local judge's office.

"They were doing 60 miles per hour in a 30-mile-per-hour speed zone," reported the policeman.

"No way! No way!" cried the motorcyclist. "I wasn't going a bit over 40 miles per hour!"

His wife chimed in, "I don't believe he was even going 40 miles per hour!"

A fellow cyclist who followed his friends to the judge's office said, "In my opinion, they were virtually at a standstill when the officer stopped them!"

The judge jumped up from his bench, raised his hands, and declared, "Stop right now before you folks back into something!"

Question: How can you tell a happy motorcyclist?

Answer: By the bugs on his teeth.

"I'm glad I passed my electrocardiogram," the cyclist said *wholeheartedly.*

Two teenagers on a bicycle-built-for-two had a tough time getting up a steep hill.

"I didn't think we'd ever make it to the top," gasped the first.

"Yes," panted the other, "and it's a good thing I kept the brakes on, or we'd a rolled right back down."

Definitions

Athlete: A dignified bunch of muscles unable to split wood or carry out the trash.

Charley Horse: A misguided muscle. A stiffness that won't do Charley or anybody else any good.

Choke: To grip farther down on the handle. To collapse under pressure. Also, what you do to an opponent who beats you by one stroke.

Class: Demonstrated not by whether you win or lose, but by how you tear up your scorecard.

Drip: A person you can always hear but seldom turn off.

"E Pluribus Unum:" A phrase that's been coined.

Fishing: Just a jerk at one end of the line waiting for a jerk at the other end.

Fox Hunting: The unspeakable in full pursuit of the uneatable.

Creative golf: Flubbing your shots with such precision that your boss actually believes he beat you fair and square.

Golf elbow: Twinges in the hinges.

"Honest" golfer: One who turns in a completely accurate scorecard 25 percent of the time.

Good friend: Anyone who doesn't play as well as you do—and does it consistently.

Green: The putting surface which contains the hole or the cup. Also, what it takes a lot of to join the club.

Guilt: Putting down your score and then wiping your fingerprints off the pencil.

Off Game: A pro's game can be "off"; yours is "just plain lousy."

Promising Athlete: Any younger player who listens attentively to your advice and nods his head in agreement.

Radical: Anyone whose opinion differs radically from yours.

A University: A football stadium surrounded by several small buildings.

Discretion is forgiving others, especially those you can't beat.

Eating

A high school football player was asked, upon ordering his pizza, if he wanted it in six or eight slices.

"Six," he replied, "I could never eat eight!"

"Give me two pounds of kidleys!" demanded the athlete on a special diet.

"I take it you mean kidneys?" asked the butcher.

He snapped back, "That's what I said, didle I?"

Your body is getting out of shape when . . . to keep you from nibbling between meals, your wife takes your teeth with her.

My waist is eighteen inches—right through the center!

Harley: "Good news and bad news about my brother's new business."

Barley: "What's the good news?"

Harley: "He opened a submarine sandwich shop."

Barley: "What's the bad news?"

Harley: "He went under."

Pro Football Player: "The airline was willing to carry all my luggage but suggested I go by bus."

Two women were talking, and one commented, "My son has two locust boys on his team at my house this weekend."

The other laughed. "That was a funny slip; you meant local, of course, dear."

"No, I said locust and I mean locust."

"But locusts—why, locusts are those insects that come in swarms, and eat up everything in sight, and . . . "

"Don't I know it," snapped her friend, "and I'm entertaining two of 'em in my home."

One player to another: "I knew him—fifty pounds ago."

"These hot dogs taste like meat at one end and

breadcrumbs at the other!" complained a patron at the ball game.

"Yes," replied the salesman, "These days it's impossible to make both ends *meat*!"

The aspirin diet: Spill a bottle of 500 aspirin on the floor every day and pick them up one at a time.

Question: Do you know why some athletes don't drink Kool-Aid?

Answer: They can't figure out how to get two quarts of water into those little packages!

The airline diet: Call an airline for reservations. You will be put on hold, and you will listen to beautiful music. If you do not eat anything until "the next available representative comes on the line" you will be well on your way to a three-day fast.

You know you are overweight when . . . the health club insists that you leave by the back door.

A grapefruit is a lemon that took advantage of its opportunities.

You need to lose weight when . . . you step on a drugstore scale and you get a card that reads, "No discounts for groups."

What you don't like or can't afford is precisely what the menu offers.

Egotism

Near miss: When you shank a golf ball out of bounds and it bounces off a car and rolls into the gutter, where it is picked up by a nearsighted crow, who then flies over the green and drops it within six inches of the cup, that's when you snap, "Another near miss."

Bragging is just a way of blowing off a little self-esteem.

A highly sought-after high school athlete was visiting a university campus. He went up to a student and asked:

"Could you tell me where the gym is at?"

"Young man," came the reply from the sophisticated student. "Never end a sentence with a preposition. It is obvious that you are still in high school."

"OK," said the high school athlete. "Can you tell me where the gym is at, stupid!"

By forgetting ourselves, we can achieve memorable goals.

During a major league ball game, the manager had to yank a pitcher. The manager walked to the mound with the bad news, but the pitcher pleaded that he be allowed to continue the game. The team was losing by five runs, and the manager was adamant.

"Why do I have to go out?" asked the pitcher.

The manager pointed to the fans and quipped, "They are beginning to talk!"

You have an ego problem when you think that your dog wags its tail only when you're out of the room.

You have no ego problems if you have no opinion about anything. You are neither for nor against apathy.

A group of golfers was telling tall stories. At last came a veteran's turn. "Well," he said, "I once drove a ball, accidentally of course, through a cottage window. The ball knocked over an oil lamp and the place caught on fire."

"What did you do?" asked his friends.

"Oh," said the veteran, "I immediately teed another ball, took careful aim and hit the fire alarm box on the street corner. That brought out the fire engines before any damage was done."

When a batter began to protest too vigorously about a called strike, the umpire whispered to him, "Quiet down, and nobody but you and me will know you can't see anymore."

A fellow from Colorado, while visiting a basketball camp in Texas, was being entertained by a Texas player. They stopped on a rather high point and the Texan bragged, "You are standing now on the highest spot in the state of Texas."

The fellow from Colorado said, "Is this as high as Pikes Peak?"

The Texan said, "Listen, man, it is a thousand miles from here to Pikes Peak and it's downhill every bit of the way."

An ego is the only thing that can keep growing without nourishment.

An outfielder was signed to play in the big leagues when he was just out of high school. When he was outfitted with a uniform, the coach asked him, "Well, son, how does it feel?"

The young fellow slid the new cap around on his head and replied awkwardly, "The cap seems a little bit too big."

The coach thundered, "See that it stays that way!"

A fisherman from a northern state was telling his host about the "big" fish he had caught while on vacation in Texas. "As a matter of fact," related the man, "I caught one that was nine inches."

The host told the fisherman that a fish that size was small even for the area around there.

"Maybe so," said the fisherman, "but down in Texas they measure a fish between the eyes."

A college athlete was invited to attend a symposium conducted by some of the nation's top space scientists. He listened attentively as the speakers read papers on various projects ranging from Mars to Venus to the moon. As the meeting progressed, the athlete finally got the attention of the scientists.

"Gentlemen, I have listened to your ideas, and

now it is time you listen to mine. I have decided to send a rocket to the sun."

"That's absurd!" shouted one scientist, "You will burn up! The heat is too much. Why, you'll fry like bacon!"

"Oh, I have the heat problem licked already. It'll go at night!"

Enthusiasm

Triumph is just umph added to try.

A pastor awoke one lovely Sunday, sniffed the morning air, and immediately began thinking of the links. As he dressed, he tried to think of his sermon and the tasks before him, but his thoughts kept slipping to those broad, green fairways. He had a service that morning, so he called his assistant and asked him to fill the pulpit.

With his clubs already in the trunk of his car, he slipped out of the house into the auto and was out on the No. 1 tee before a soul noticed he was missing.

"I'm in luck," he thought, as he took a few practice swings. "There isn't another person on the course."

Looking down from heaven, St. Peter wagged his finger. "Shame! Just look at that," he said. "A man of the cloth playing golf on the Lord's Day when he has work at the church!"

Just then the pastor lifted a beautiful 300-yard drive right down the center of the long fairway. The ball sailed to the edge of the green, bounced once, twice, three times, rolled, and disappeared into the cup. The pastor leaped for joy.

"Disgusting!" exclaimed St. Peter. "He made a hole in one! Is that right to allow such a thing?"

Then St. Peter reasoned: "On second thought, who can he tell?"

During a ball game, a reporter in the press box put his topcoat over the railing. During the game the coat slipped and landed on a fan below. The fan looked up and called, "Where's the pants?"

The father of a Little League baseball player arrived as the teams were locked in battle. He approached his son on the bench and asked, "What's the score?"

"Twenty-eight to nothing."

"Good heavens!" muttered the father, "Twenty-eight to zero. Boy, that's real bad!"

"Oh, no, it's not," said the kid. "We haven't gotten our bat yet."

A man with a balky mule had done all he could think of to budge that mule. The country doctor came along and said he had something that would start the mule.

"Give it to him," the farmer said. "I'm worn out!"

The doctor pulled out a long needle and gave the mule a shot. In a few minutes the mule perked up and dashed off at a mad run.

The farmer watched the cloud of dust the mule left behind. "How much of that stuff did you give him?" he asked.

"Oh, about a dollar's worth," the doctor answered.

"Well, Doc, give me three dollars worth. I've got to catch him."

Four-letter words:

Game! Golf! Putt! Hole! Club! Flag! Ball! Cart! Sand! Trap! Brag! These common four-letter words inevitably lead to even more common four-letter words.

During a football game, one of the backs on the opposing team ripped through the line time and time again, until the ball was within a few yards of the goal line. On the next play the same back again tore through the line, shaking off one man after another, and at the goal line was finally brought down by several defensive players precisely as the timer's gun sounded.

"My goodness!" shouted a spectator. "They had to shoot him to stop him!"

A wife told a counselor, "I think my husband really loves me. The other afternoon he was watching football, so I got up on a ladder to change a light bulb. I fell off and broke my leg."

"What makes you think he loves you?"

"He didn't wait until halftime to call the doctor."

The annual football game between two rival high schools was being played. As one team would score, a spectator cheered and threw his hat high in the air. When the other team scored, this same spectator was equally delighted. This puzzled the man in the next seat, so he asked, "Which side are you rooting for, my good man?"

"Who, me?" replied the excited cheerer. "Oh, I'm not supporting either side. I'm just here to enjoy the game."

Four men were on the golf course and had just reached the eighth hole, which was next to a highway. As the men moved onto the green, a funeral procession passed along the road. One of the men removed his cap and stood solemnly as the procession passed by. One of his friends was touched by this gesture of respect and said so.

"Oh, it's the least I could do," replied the man. "In five more days we would have been married twenty-six years." Yecch!

Fear

A pilot took his friend for an airplane ride.

"I want a thrill," the man said.

The pilot rolled the plane; he did figures in the sky. Finally, he nose dived almost to the earth and swept back into the air again.

"Did you see those people?" the pilot asked excitedly. "About 50 percent of them thought we were going to land on them."

"That's nothing," his friend gasped. "Fifty percent of the people up here thought so too."

A pitcher had a blazing fastball. The batter struck a match above his head, but the umpire said to quit messing around and put it out.

The batter replied, "But I want to make sure this pitcher sees me."

You fear only fear itself when you can walk into an empty room and start an argument.

Ted: "One should not fear flying. The Bible says, 'I am with you always.'"

Todd:"But reread the passage, it says, '*Lo,* I am with you always.' "

One major league manager forbade his pitchers to throw a strike when the count was zero and two. He'd fine them $500.

Once, a rookie reliever had two strikes on the batter. Mindful of the manager's rule, he prepared to waste a ball. Instead, it clipped the corner and the ump called "strike three!" The rookie pitcher ran in from the mound and started screaming at the ump.

"That was a ball. Are you trying to get me in trouble with my manager?"

A major league pitcher was feared by all opposing teams. His fastball was so fast he could throw it through a car wash and not get a drop of water on it!

Fishing

Old fishermen never die; they just smell that way!

Definition of a guy who loves to fish: a *finatic!*

One day a parishioner presented his pastor a fine catch of brook trout, but said hesitantly, "Sir, I guess I ought to tell you that these trout were caught on a camping trip last Sunday."

The pastor gazed hungrily at them and declared, "Well, the trout aren't to blame. Thanks for them."

Fish hooks have really caught on.

A fisherman watched as a grizzled old guide in an adjoining boat carefully cut a fishing line part way through, a few inches above the gaily colored lure.

"Why are you doing that?" He asked, mystified.

"I'm fixin' to take an amateur out purty soon. He'll likely snag a fair fish. When he goes to lift 'im into the boat, the line'll break. That feller will tell all his friends about the big 'un that got away."

The old man looked about slyly, then added confidentially, "What's more, he'll come back here every summer for the rest of his life trying to catch 'im."

Angler: A man who spends rainy days sitting around on the muddy banks of rivers doing nothing because his wife won't let him do it at home.

A fellow was walking along a country road after a hard rainstorm when he came upon a fellow sitting in an easy chair by the kitchen door, fishing in a puddle of water.

The fellow asked the man what he was doing there.

"Fishin' a little," replied the man.

"Well, don't you know there are no fish there?"

"Yes, Sir," said the man, "I know that, but this place is so handy."

A fish probably goes home and lies about the size of the bait he stole.

Identical twins, known as Harry and Bob, were indefatigable fishermen. The difference was that Bob always caught fish, but Harry never did. It was inexplicable. One morning Harry and Bob changed clothes completely, from waders to fly-ringed hats. Harry made a long, upstream cast. As the fly floated down, up rose a trout, who gave one disdainful look at the fisherman and asked, "Where's Bob?"

A man will sit in a spot without catching a fish for hours and then raise the dickens if his wife is a few minutes late fixing dinner.

A fishing tackle salesman reached into his sample case and drew forth a gaudy lure, striped, spotted, and colorful. His friend eyed it cautiously and asked: "Do you sell many of those? I wouldn't think a bass would go for such an awful contraption."

"Best lure there is," said the salesman with a grin. "You see, I don't sell 'em to the bass—just to the suckers."

"Help, I can't swim! I can't swim!" cried a fellow in the water.

"I can't either," said an old man, sitting on the bank fishing. "But I'm not hollerin' about it."

A boy who had been playing hooky from school, had spent a long, leisurely day fishing. On his way back he met one of his young cronies who asked, "Catch anything?"

"Ain't been home yet," he replied.

Football

Noticing that prior to the football game, both teams gathered together and prayed briefly, a fan seated next to a preacher asked what he thought would happen if both teams prayed with equal faith and fervor.

"In that event," replied the preacher, "I imagine the Lord would simply sit back and enjoy one fine game of football."

Have you ever noticed how the football uniforms get fancier as the team gets worse?

Question: "What do you call a football player with keen intuition?"
Answer: "A *hunchback.*"

All during the skull sessions preceding the big game, one of the star backs spent most of the time reading a joke book (to the mounting fury of the coach). But the coach said nothing.

On the day of the game, this particular back sat on the bench until late in the last quarter when the situation began to get critical. The coach called to him and said, "Warm up!" The star player jumped up and went through a series of warm-ups, then turned expectantly towards the coach.

"Here," snarled the coach as he pulled a joke book out of his pocket. "Sit over there at the end of the bench and read it."

Visitor at college campus to husky college student wearing varsity sweater: "What university is this?"
Student: "I don't know, Sir. I just play football here."

Did you ever hear about the football coach who had to resign because of the severe persecution complex he developed? Every time his players went into a huddle, the coach thought they were talking about him.

A foreign student's observation at his first football game was: it was a "shameful inadequacy of American production. If each boy had a football, there would be no reason to fight over it."

An outstanding football coach kept substitutes

on the bench constantly alert by suddenly popping questions at them while a game was in progress.

One game, he turned to a third-string sub who had played the role of human tackling dummy in practice all season and demanded: "What would you do if we had possession of the ball, one minute to play, the score nothing to nothing, and we had only five yards to go for a touchdown?"

"Gee, coach," stammered the substitute, "I'd slide down to the end of the bench, so I could see better."

"I'm not saying he's dumb, but when he won his varsity letter, somebody had to read it to him!" snapped the coach.

A pastor announced, "I've made up my mind never to attend another football game. I've been an avid football fan for many years, but now I've had it." Then he listed the reasons why:

1. I was taken to too many games by my parents when I was growing up.
2. The games are always played when I want to do something else.
3. Every time I go to a game, somebody asks for money.

4. Although I go to games quite often, few people are friendly enough to speak to me.
5. The seats are too hard and uncomfortable. Besides, I often have to sit down front on the fifty yard line.
6. I suspect there are hypocrites sitting nearby. They come to see their friends and to look at what others are wearing rather than to see the game.
7. The field judge says things with which I don't agree.
8. The band usually plays some numbers I've never heard before.
9. Some games last too long, making me get home late.
10. I have a good book on football. I can stay home and read that.

Then he concluded: "Well, there they are—ten reasons why I will never attend another football game. Kind of foolish, isn't it, to miss the joy of football for reasons like these? I wonder how many of us are missing the joys of church for reasons just as foolish?"

Football is a clean sport because it's about the only one with "scrub" teams.

The fullback bragged to his coach:

"Did you see me run across the goal line five times that half?"

"Yeah, you arrowhead," shouted the coach, "but it only counts when you have the ball."

"Shucks," muttered the fullback, "every year, new rules."

"What position does your son play on the football team, Mrs. Smith?"

"I'm not sure," replied Mrs. Smith, "but I think he's one of the *drawbacks.*"

A confused quarterback signaled for a fair catch when the center snapped the ball.

Referee: What a football player becomes after he loses his eyesight.

Most colleges are installing artificial turf on their football fields—cost about $300,000, but one local college paid $400,000.

Reason: They're including an underground sprinkler system.

Golf

Deep in the weeds: When you're so far out in the rough the club secretary asks you to fill out a change-of-address card.

Bill and Joe were beginning a game of golf. Bill stepped up to his tee, and his first drive gave him a hole in one. Joe stepped up to the tee and said, "OK, now I'll take my practice swing, and then we'll start the game."

A businessman who frequently left the office to play golf instructed his secretary to tell all callers that he was away from his desk. After he left the office, a member of his foursome forgot which course they were playing that day, so he called for information. The loyal secretary would only reply that her boss was away from his desk.

"Just tell me," the golfer persisted, "Is he ten miles away from his desk, or twenty miles?"

Nothing is more discouraging than playing with a golfer who is so good he doesn't have to cheat.

A preacher was engaged in a closely contested game of golf. He teed up to his ball, raised his driver, and hit the ball a tremendous clip, but instead of soaring down the fairway, the ball went less than twenty feet. The cleric pursed his mouth, bit his lips, sighed, but said nothing.

One of the other players turned to him and said, "That was the most profane silence I have ever heard."

A golfer can accept advice gracefully—if it doesn't interfere with what he intended to do in the first place.

Pro shop: Only place in the world where you can buy a purple cap, pink-and-green-checked slacks, and an orange shirt embroidered with blue palm trees—and still be considered the conservatively dressed member of your foursome.

A golfer, who had made a real bad shot and tore up a large piece of turf, took the sod in his hand and asked: "What shall I do with this?"

"If I were you," shot back the caddy, "I'd take it home to practice on."

The church choir director was playing golf one day. Every time he swung a club, the ball went wild. His exasperation mounted by the minute, until finally he asked his caddy, "What am I doing wrong? What's the matter with me?"

Replied the astute caddy, "Mister, you just ain't got rhythm."

Greg: "Did you know that Ferdinand Magellan went around the world in 1521?"

Gene: "That isn't too many strokes when you consider the distance."

A priest played his first round of golf and enjoyed it so thoroughly he became a fanatic on the subject. Finally the bishop had to send for him.

"My son," said the bishop, "I have always encouraged healthful exercise, and I consider golf both an excellent diversion and a means of communing with nature. But if one plays golf too much, one is apt to neglect his real duties."

The father was crushed. "May I ask why you seem to think I am overdoing it?" he asked humbly.

"I noticed," said the bishop gently, "that when you approached the altar this morning you were holding your prayer book with a famous golf grip."

You can always tell a golf enthusiast by the fairway look in his eyes.

A fellow who took up golf wasn't doing too well with it. Finally, one day he came home and told his wife he finally had a winning day.

"I'm so happy for you," she said. "Did you make a birdie?"

"Not exactly—but I found more golf balls that I lost."

Hole: A round receptacle in the green, four inches in diameter. The golf hole is the only thing in the world that gets smaller as you get closer to it.

Hole-in-one: A mixed blessing that brings joy and frustration. For the rest of your life you'll never be able to do better on that particular hole.

Bill: "Why is golf a lot like taxes?"

Bob: "Because you drive very hard to get to the green, and then you wind up in the hole!"

"I'd move heaven and earth to break 100," said the golf addict as he desperately banged away in a sand trap.

"Try heaven," advised his partner. "You've already moved enough earth."

"Sorry I can't take any more appointments today," said the dentist to a patient on the phone, "I already have eighteen cavities to fill."

Then he hung up the phone, picked up his golf bag, and left.

A newspaper ad read: "Must sell golf clubs—or get a divorce."

Bermuda: Grass used on some golf courses. When it comes to watching balls sink out of sight, golfers have their own Bermuda Triangle.

"You think so much about your golf game that

you don't even remember when we were married," complained the wife.

"Sure I do; it was the day I sank that 37-yard putt."

A golfer is one who totes twenty-five pounds of equipment several miles, but has his wife bring him a glass of ice tea.

Caddy: A person who carries a player's clubs and often keeps score. A good one understands that less is more.

Celebrity: A lousy golfer who gets to play in a lot of tournaments nonetheless.

Celebrity match: Where everybody is somebody, so nobody is anybody.

Charity tournament: A philanthropic event. A fun way to help the less fortunate—as long as it is tax-deductible.

Divot: A piece of turf cut out by a club head during a bad stroke. As a rule, the ball should go farther than the divot.

Duffer: A golfer who is not having as much fun on weekends as his wife thinks he is.

Fairway: Well-kept portion of ground between tee and putting green. We include this because many golfers have never seen it.

Fringe: Grass area that immediately borders the putting surface. Also called the apron, and you know how easy it is to mess up an apron.

Grounds committee: A duly elected group which dedicates itself to one ultimate goal—Neglect.

Group behind: Foursome behind you. They creep up on you like cheap underwear.

Lost ball: The quickest way to find a lost ball is to put a new one into play.

Obstacles: Bunkers, sand traps, water holes, but most of all—you.

Refrigeration theory: Golf balls will last longer if kept in a refrigerator. They will last longer only if never taken out of the refrigerator.

Scorecard: When blank: an innocent piece of paper. When filled: a blankety, blank, blank . . .

Tournament: A competition in either match or stroke play. Those who can play—play. Those who cannot, get a tournament named after them.

Whisper: The modulated voice of a TV golf announcer who pretends the golfer shooting on the 16th fairway can hear him in the booth at the 18th green.

The pro was lecturing a particularly slow student. "Now look, you've got to keep your eye on the ball at all times."

The duffer answered, "I did last time, and somebody stole my golf cart."

"What's your golf score?" the recreation director asked.

"Well, not so good," replied the golfer. "It's 73."

"That's not so bad at all. In fact, it's real good."

"Well, I'm hoping to do better *on the next hole*," said the golfer.

A little girl watching a golfer in a sand trap said to her mother, "He's stopped beating it, Mother. I think it must be dead."

Joe says his golf is improving—the other day he hit a ball in one.

Hockey

He waited outside the hockey arena for his wife. She was more than an hour late, and when she finally arrived he was so angry he could hardly speak. Silently, he bought the tickets and they went in.

"What's the score?" she asked.

"Nothing to nothing," he answered.

"There, you see," she declared. "We haven't missed a thing!"

A professional hockey coach asked the team's owner, "Would you have liked me as much if we had lost?"

The owner replied, "Yes, but I would have missed you."

Two Greeks were in Dublin, Ireland, watching a game of Irish field hockey.

"Do you understand this game?" asked one of them.

"No I don't," said the second Greek, "It's all Irish to me!"

Returning to his seat at a hockey game with popcorn and a soft drink, the student leaned over the woman at the end of the row and asked: "Excuse me, did I step on your feet when I went out?"

"Yeah!" came the reply.

"Good, I was afraid this wasn't the right row."

A college hockey team was being badly beaten by a lower-rated team. Between periods the team had sadly sat in the dressing room awaiting the coach's inevitable thunder. Only silence came.

Shortly before time to go onto the ice for resumption of play the coach came in. He stood at the threshold, glanced swiftly over the players, bowed gently but unsmiling, then turned and left as he said over his shoulder, "I beg your pardon, children, but I thought this was our men's college hockey team."

The losing team of a close hockey game was disappointed with the referee's calls. One player on the team went to a referee after the game and said, "It was really a good game. It's too bad you didn't get to see it as it was played!"

Hunting

A father and his small son were out duck hunting. Dad bragged on how good a shot he was. Then a lone duck flew over, the father took careful aim, and fired. The duck kept right on flying.

The father was not upset. He turned to the boy and said, "Son, you have just witnessed a miracle? There flies a dead duck."

Butcher: "I'm sorry, but we have no ducks today. How about a nice leg of lamb?"

Hunter: "Don't be silly. I can't tell my wife I shot a leg of lamb, can I?"

The members of a hunting party had been specifically requested to bring only male hounds. One indigent member, however, owned only a female, and out of courtesy was finally permitted to include her. The pack was off in a flash. In a matter of seconds they were completely out of sight. The confused hunters stopped to question a farmer in a nearby field. "Did you see some hounds go by here?"

"Yep," said the farmer.

"See where they went?"

"Nope," was the reply, "but it was the first time I ever seen a fox running fourth!"

I went frog hunting and came home very *hoppy.*

A deer hunter arrived for his third season at a hunting resort and began unpacking his suitcase—carefully and neatly arranged by his wife.

She obviously had little faith in her husband's deer-hunting ability. On the top layer he found a drawing of a deer and, in his wife's handwriting, the helpful message:

"Here's what one looks like."

Jerry: "Did you hear about the hunter who lost his dog in the woods?"

Joe: "No, how did he find him?"

Jerry: "He put his ear to a tree and listened to the bark!"

A sportsman whose previous activity was big game hunting decided to take on the game of golf. During his first game he managed to hit one magnificent long drive. He couldn't resist boasting about that particular shot.

"Wasn't that drive marvelous?" he badgered a friend for the umpteenth time.

"It certainly was," huffed the friend, "it's a pity you can't have it stuffed."

A famous lawyer also enjoyed big game hunting. From one such trip he did not return. It was feared that something he disagreed with ate him.

Two hunters on a safari encountered a lion, but the lion fooled them. Instead of standing his ground and fighting, the lion escaped into the underbrush. One of the terrified hunters finally stammered to his friend, "You go ahead and see where he went. I'll backtrack and see where he came from."

A minister visited a couple he had recently married. The wife was crying when he arrived, and the minister asked the reason.

"My husband's gone out to shoot some golf, and I don't know how to cook 'em."

Old Roscoe was trained to catch rabbits by size. His owner would show the dog a small skin-stretching board, and the dog would bring back a small rabbit. If he saw the large board, the dog brought back a large rabbit. One day someone left the ironing board on the front porch, and the old hound hasn't been seen since.

"All right, who stole my thermal underwear?" the hunter shouted *coldly*.

The game warden was strolling through the mountains when he encountered a hunter with a gun. "This is fine territory for hunting, don't you think?" the warden asked.

"You bet it is," replied the hunter enthusiastically. "I killed one of the biggest bucks you ever saw yesterday. Must have weighed at least 200 pounds."

"Deer are out of season now," said the warden. "Do you know you are talking to a game warden?"

"No, I didn't know that," said the hunter. "And I'll bet you didn't know that you've been talking to the biggest liar in the state."

"Our best dog lost a front leg in a fight with a

boar, and we made him a wooden leg," said the old timer.

"But, you know, it kind of spoiled our hunting, 'cause every time the dog cornered an animal he'd hit it over the head with that wooden leg. It took a lot of the fun out of hunting for me!"

Jogging

An exhausted jogger can detect an uphill grade so insignificant that it would be missed by most surveyors.

No matter how fast you run, you always get trapped in the middle of the intersection when the signal changes to "Don't Walk."

The jogger's greatest hazard has a collar, four legs, and an owner who swears, "I don't understand, he's never bitten anyone before."

Dogs, who fondly lick the hands of cat burglars, become canine psychopaths when they think a runner is threatening their turf.

Moe: "A local health spa installed an indoor coin-operated jogging machine."

Joe: "Why?"

Moe: "They wanted to give their clients a run for their money."

You are eating too much when you have more jiggle than jog when you run.

A famous runner has calculated that when he runs a marathon (26 miles, 385 yards), the length of his stride is approximately 36 inches or one yard. This means he must lift his body off the ground 46,145 times. And each time he puts a foot down, it absorbs the equivalent of three times his body weight, which is 150 pounds, for a total weight of (body weight x 3) 450 pounds. So over the course of a marathon, his feet must bear a total weight of (46,145 x 450)—20,765,000 pounds! This translates (divide by 2,000) to over 10,382 tons!

With this figure in mind, if your stride is approximately one yard, note what you must lift if you run a marathon:

Your Weight	Tons
100	6,922
110	7,614
120	8,306
130	8,998
140	9,609
150	10,382
160	11,075
170	11,767
180	12,459
190	13,151

That's why I don't jog. It makes me tired just thinking about it!

A woman asked her friend, "Does your husband take any special exercise?"

The friend replied, "Last week he was out seven nights running."

You know you have taken jogging too seriously when:

    ... your mate says, "Would you mind running this package over to the post office for me?" and you never consider taking the car.

    ... you write an angry letter complaining that you got only 12,000 miles out of your last pair of tennis shoes.

    ... you miss a day of running, and it causes you more guilt than forgetting your Mother's birthday.

    ... the manager of your full-service bank gives you an ultimatum. "Stop doing stretching exercises while you're waiting in line, or we'll start bouncing your checks!"

    ... despite what your mate thinks, you can carry on a conversation about something other than running—as long as the listener is moving at the same pace you are.

. . . you won't let your pet cat sleep on the bed, because when it comes to oxygen, you won't share with anyone.

You know you have courage when the salesgirl at your local shoe store will only sell you jogging shoes if you promise not to tell anyone where you purchased them.

Obesity

You know you are off your diet when you get your shoes shined and you have to take the guy's word for it.

Middle age: When dangerous curves become extended detours.

You know you need to trim up when you look in the mirror and notice you're breaking out in hips.

Obesity: Surplus gone to waist.

There is something to be said in defense of fat: it's one of the few things people can still accumulate.

Overheard in the locker room: "I went on a diet for two weeks and all I lost was fourteen days."

Have you heard about the fellow who had so much flab on him that when he stands up, his feet disappear?

He was crossing the street the other day and was hit by a small foreign car. They don't think there was any serious damage. Of course, they still haven't found the car.

There was a man so large that the day he wore a green shirt with white stripes, a bunch of kids played football on him.

You know you are getting too heavy when the only way you can get out of a phone booth is back out.

The 100% Oil Diet

You eat nothing but peanut oil, corn oil, and sunflower oil. You don't lose any weight but you never squeak.

The Good Taste Diet

If it tastes good, spit it out.

You have a weight problem when your mouth has developed stretch marks.

You have a weight problem when your clothes start to hurt.

How Athletes Can Stay Thin

To appear thinner, only hang out with fat people.

Run every place you go. If you don't lose weight, it will at least keep you from being mugged.

Eat all you want of the food you can't stand.

For dinner, have a two-pound steak. This will give you the strength to diet tomorrow.

If nothing else works, try acupuncture. Maybe you can get it to leak out.

One person would not admit to gaining a lot of weight, but his doctor put him on industrial-strength diet pills.

Coach: "Why haven't you lost any weight?"

Player: "Well, to be honest, I haven't watched my diet in a month of sundaes!"

Pain

"I suppose this means you've won the sword fight," he said *pointedly.*

A rookie with a pro football team was eager to get into a game as a pass receiver, and day after day practiced catching balls thrown by quarterbacks. But time passed, and still the earnest rookie failed to receive word from the coach.

Finally, during the last quarter of a game the rookie was told to prepare for going into the game. Just before leaving the bench he turned for instructions. "We've run out of timeouts," said the coach. "Go in there and get hurt."

Patient to acupuncturist: "That's a jab well done!"

A very rich man suddenly clutched his heart and yelled to his wife, "I think I'm gonna have a heart attack!" Exasperated, he ordered his wife, "Well, don't just stand there. Buy me a hospital!"

"I've just swallowed an entire window," the woman shouted *panefully.*

Jack: "Did you hear about the glassblower who inhaled instead of exhaling?"
Joe: "No, what happened?"
Jack: "He got a pane in his stomach!"

Imagining himself to be the ancient thunder god Thor, the Viking ran out and jumped on a horse. After galloping about for an hour he cried, "I'm Thor!"

The horse replied, "You forgot the thaddle, thilly!"

A preacher, vacationing at a dude ranch, wanted to ride a horse.

"We've got just the horse for you to ride, parson," said the ranch foreman.

"He has been trained different from most horses. He don't know 'Giddyup' and 'Whoa.'

"Because we saved him for church folk, we trained him to listen to other commands. If you say, 'Praise the Lord,' he'll take off like a streak of lightning. But if you want him to stop, just say 'Amen.' "

The minister was pleased. As he mounted, he said, "Praise the Lord!" The horse leaped forward and ran fast. It was grand, zestful riding; soon the horse was going at a rapid pace.

This dude ranch was right on top of a mountain, and just yonder a quarter of a mile away was a sheer drop-off of 2,000 feet—straight down!

And lo! The preacher discovered that his horse was galloping right toward that cliff. Eternity was staring him in the face.

The poor man panicked so he couldn't think of the word to make the horse stop. But finally it came to him, and he shouted "AMEN!"

Scree-e-e-e-ech! The horse responded—dug his hooves in, skidded right to the very edge of the cliff where his head hung over.

The thankful preacher exhaled, looked up to heaven, put a hand to his brow, and yelled, "Praise the Lord!"

An old racetrack fan was asked why he had refused to contribute to a statue honoring Paul Revere. "Why," he said, "Revere doesn't deserve any credit. He just had a terrific horse under him."

A man asked a rancher, "You got any fast horses on your ranch?"

"Ah got the fastest horse in the state," said the rancher.

"One day, I was fifty miles from my spread when a storm came up. I turned the pony's head for home, and he raced the storm so close that for the last ten miles I didn't feel a drop. . . .

"But my dog, who was only ten yards behind at first, had to swim the whole distance."

Question: If rubber-soled sneakers are worn in basketball and leather shoes in bowling, in what sport are all-metal shoes worn?

Answer: Horse racing.

Rodeo

A rodeo cowboy retires when his legs buckle . . . but his belt won't!

Larry: "Why in the world would cowboys compete in rodeos?"

Barry: "Well, they get a few bucks out of it."

Two cowboys were examining a flagpole at the rodeo grounds and were shaking their heads from side to side.

"What's your trouble?" asked an interested bystander.

One of the cowboys said, "We can't figure out how tall this flagpole is."

To help the two cowboys out, the fellow lifted the flagpole out of its concrete base, laid it on the ground, took out his tape, and proceeded to measure it.

The two cowboys exclaimed, "That won't help us a bit! We wanted to know how tall it is, not how long it is!"

An irate cowboy in town for the rodeo bellowed

into the phone at the small hotel, "Are you the desk clerk of this dilapidated joint?"

"Yes, I am. What's eating you?" asked the clerk.

"That's exactly what I'd like to know!"

Skiing

Skier: A guy who jumps to contusions!

A weatherman near a popular ski resort was fired from the local TV station because his weather reports never seemed to be accurate.

"I'll be glad to get out of this town anyway. The weather doesn't agree with me!" he snorted.

Did you hear about the girl who learned to ski in just ten sittings?

Skiing Mania—Sloping Sickness!

A man learning to ski said, "By the time I learned to stand up, I couldn't sit down."

Skiing: Whoosh! Then walk a mile.

Soccer

One soccer player takes a cold shower after every game—after all the other players have taken hot ones.

A soccer player went to a doctor complaining, "I feel like a small, flat biscuit."

"There's no such thing as a small, flat biscuit," said the doctor, "Do you feel like you are small and square?"

"Yes!" said the patient.

"Why, you're not a biscuit at all," came back the doctor, "You're crackers!"

A soccer player seeing the high salaries of football players said, "It's no disgrace to be poor, but it's mighty inconvenient."

A soccer player and a football player went to play golf. The soccer player repeatedly tore up more turf than golf balls and sent the dirt flying after every stroke. Finally he asked the football player how he liked the golf course.

"Best I ever tasted," said the football player, wiping dirt off his face.

Soccer player: "What do I do if I hurt my foot?"
Doctor: "Limp!"

Success

A college football star had gone in for some fancy footwork and showboating during a game. He was repeatedly thrown for losses by a player on the opposing team. When he was taken from the game, the dismayed star sat on the bench, turned to the coach, and said, "I'm sorry I messed things up. I had no idea that guy was so fast and smart."

"Oh, it's not your fault," said the coach. "You should have just shown him your press clippings —then he wouldn't have dared put a hand on you."

Rules

1. The coach is always right.
2. When the coach is wrong, refer to Rule 1.

The dictionary is the only place where success comes before work.

He was showing off his handsome new home. They walked into the spacious living room, featuring antique furniture and mahogany paneling.

Then, the host leaned out the window and shouted,

"Green side up!"

Then, they walked into a den, complete with pool table and Ping Pong table. And, again, the host moved to the window and said, "Green side up!"

They went into a bathroom, which featured a sunken tub; then into a kitchen with all the latest appliances. And, again, the host went to the window and called, "Green side up!"

"Excuse me," said his guest. "You certainly have a beautiful house. But why do you keep going to the various windows and shouting, "Green side up?"

"Oh," explained the host, "I have four of our high school athletes outside sodding the lawn."

Anyone can win—unless there happens to be a second entry.

You know a man is successful when the newspapers start quoting him on subjects he knows nothing about.

Two of the most difficult things in this world are

making a name for yourself, and second, keeping it.

There are three ways to get something done: do it yourself, hire someone, or forbid your kids to do it.

Success is one's ability to make more money to meet obligations one wouldn't have if one didn't have so much money.

Letter From Athlete To Former Teacher

Dear Sir: you never past me in grammer because you was prejudice but I got this here athaletic scolership any ways. Wel, the other day I finely get to writing the rules of good grammer down so as I can always study it if they ever slips my mine. My rule's is:
Don't aabbrev.
About sentence fragmints.
Don't use no double negetives.
Check to see if you any words out.
When dangling, don't use participales.
Verbs has to agree with their subjects.
Its important to use apostrophe's right.

Don't use commers, which arent necessary.

Just between you and I, case is important.

Each pronoun agrees with their antycedent.

A riter mustnt shif your point of view.

Join clawses good like conjunctions should.

As far as incomplet cornstructions, they are wrong.

Don't rite a run-on sentence you got to punktuate it.

In the case of a business letter, check it in terms of jargon.

Watch out for irreguler varbs which has creped into the langwige.

About repetition, the repetition of a word might be reel effective repetition.

In letters themes reports artikles and stuff like that we use commers to keep a strang of itims apart.

In my opionion I think that an arthur when he is riting shouldn't get into the habit of making use of too many unnecessary words that he does not really need in order to put his message across.

Last, but not leest, lay off cliches.

A young woman at her first baseball game said she liked the pitcher best, "Because he almost always hits the bat."

Swimming

Two upbeat fellows were swimming. The unskilled swimmer suddenly slipped into a deep hole. Floundering in the water, he yelled to his partner, "Hey, man, how about giving me a hand?"

On hearing this, the partner began applauding loudly.

A swimmer, suffering from stomach pains, went to a doctor. The doctor, a rather weird sort of fellow, suggested that the swimmer remove the thong from his right foot and chew off and swallow an inch of it each day for the next thirty days.

After thirty days the athlete returned to the doctor.

"How are you feeling?" Asked the doctor.

"The thong is ended but the malady lingers on," replied the swimmer.

One should be careful to keep his mouth shut—when swimming and when angry.

A college student tried out for the college swim team and failed to make it.

During his senior year, he went to the swimming coach and asked why he'd never been selected for the team.

"Confidentially," the coach whispered, "You sink!"

A woman swimming in the ocean couldn't make it back to shore and yelled for help.

A man jumped into the water to save her. He grabbed for her hair, and her wig came off. He grabbed for her feet, and her artificial leg came off. He made a life-saver's grab at her mouth, and her teeth came out.

"Hey, lady," he yelled. "If you want me to save you, you've gotta cooperate a little bit!"

An ideal swimmer's resort would be where the fish bite and the mosquitoes don't.

Sunbathing: A fry in the ointment!

A great swimmer had won many titles and was in the habit of swimming in the Atlantic Ocean early every morning before reporting for his job. He sometimes would spot a solitary person walking along the beach. He would then swim to the shore and call out, "What town is this?"

"New York," the startled pedestrian would reply.

"Oh, I want Miami," the swimmer would call out and then plunge back into the water and swim away.

A swimming pool is a crowd of people with water in it.

Tennis

A tennis court is the only place in the world where love means nothing.

An elderly former tennis great retired to a little house with her favorite friends—cats.

"I own twenty cats," bragged the little old lady.

"I guess that requires an awful lot of care and special attention at your house," exclaimed a friend.

"Yes, I've had to drill twenty holes in the front door of my house so the cats can get out to the yard."

"Twenty holes!" exclaimed her friend. "You could just drill one hole and they could exit single file."

"I guess I could," said the little old lady. "But when I say scat! I mean *SCAT!*"

Question: Is tennis mentioned in the Bible?

Answer: Yes, when Joseph served in Pharaoh's court.

A tennis pro was asked by reporters what he did for relaxation. He answered, "I shoot golf in the low 70s. When it gets any colder, I quit."

Track

Even if you are on the right track, you will get run over if you just sit there.

When the college track team was called out for the first practice session of the season, one of the aspirants was so fleet of foot that he made the others look like snails. The coach called him over and asked him how he developed such incredible speed.

"I used to catch jackrabbits on my pa's farm," he explained.

"But," the coach pointed out, "a lot of other boys here claim they did the same thing. But they're not nearly as fast as you."

"Well, my dad is pretty fussy about the rabbits he eats," the boy elaborated. "I had to run 'long side of them and feel them to see if they were fat enough for my father before I caught them."

Question: "Know what happened to the javelin thrower who sat on his javelin?"

Answer: "He got the point!"

Four students were standing under one umbrella at a track meet.

"This is terrific!" marveled one of them. "All of us under one umbrella and none of us are getting wet."

"Probably because it isn't raining," observed a passerby.

Larry: "Do you know what they call a long-distance runner?"

Harry: "No, what?"

Larry: "A landscape *panter!*"

A track star was to appear in court as a witness in a civil suit. "Are you on the track team this year?" asked the judge.

"Yes, Your Honor."

"What do you run?"

"The 200-yard dash, Your Honor."

"How good a runner are you?"

The runner squirmed in his chair, but in confident tones admitted, "Sir, I'm the best runner this college ever had."

The coach heard about this statement and was surprised because the runner was always modest and unassuming. The coach later asked the runner why he had made such a statement.

"I hated to, Coach, but I had no choice. I was under oath."

A cross-country runner, suffering from a sudden spell of dizziness, stopped to sit a minute with his head resting on his knees.

"Have you vertigo?" asked a curious passerby.

"Yes! Two more miles," he said.

Weather

A foreign potentate loved animals so he forbade any of his subjects to kill them. The animals became so numerous that all the crops in the country were destroyed. The potentate was deposed from his throne because of his order. That was the first time in history that the reign was called on account of game.

In sports—to have a place in the sun for yourself, you have to be a shade better than the next fellow.

"The smog is really bad today," he cried *breathlessly*.

A baseball manager wanted the game called because of approaching darkness. There were no lights at the field.

The umpire refused and ordered the game to continue. A few minutes later, the manager used a flashlight to signal the bullpen to send in a new pitcher, for which the manager was thrown out of the game.

Witticisms

He who lives by the crystal ball will soon learn to eat broken glass.

What is the meaning of the word "wise?"
It is used by most children as, "Wise the sky blue?"

If you have to ask, you're not entitled to know. If you don't like the answer, you shouldn't have asked in the first place.

Ben: "Do you know why he was able to see the glacier before anyone else?"
Bob: "No, why?"
Ben: "He had good ice sight."

Two-handicap golfer: A player with a boss who won't let him take off early, and a wife who keeps him home on weekends.

"You know what makes me jumpy?"

"No, what?"
"A pogo stick."

Misery no longer loves company. Nowadays it insists on it.

Naivete: The assumption that you're going to be using the same ball after 18 holes of golf.

Good judgment comes from experience, and experience comes from poor judgment.

Putt: The shortest shot which takes the longest time.

Quitting golf: In order to be smart enough to quit golf, you had to be dumb enough to start.

Think twice before you speak—especially if you intend to say what you think.

The farther away from the entrance of the game

(theater, or any other given location) that you have to park, the closer the space vacated by the car that pulls away as you walk up to the door.

Just when you finally figure out where it's at . . . somebody moves it!

Never insult an alligator until after you have crossed the river.

Question: What happened to the water polo team?
Answer: The horses drowned.

Early rising is due to the triumph of mind over mattress.

What do you get if you cross a tree with a baseball player who hit a lot of home runs?
Babe Root. Yeecchh!

Two ladies were talking about their sons. One

asked the other, "What position does your son play on the football team?"

"I'm not sure, but I think he's one of the drawbacks."

Colleges sometimes have an end in view when lowering the entrance requirements—or a halfback or quarterback or . . .

When a famous catcher was a rookie in spring-training camp, measurements were being taken for uniforms, and he was asked his cap size.

"How do I know?" replied the catcher. "I'm not in shape yet."

Time Out (Miscellaneous)

Guest Lecturer: "Ladies and gentlemen, I know you're wondering how I got this cast. Well, if there are any of you out there who have just bought the latest book on *Exercising at Home,* there's a misprint on page 204."

Karate Teacher: What hurts worse than a karate chop in the chest?
Student: One of my mom's pork chops in the stomach.

They say that it will soon be possible to fly around the world in three hours—one hour to get around the world and two hours to get out of the airport parking lot.

If you feel dogtired, it's probably because you have growled all day.

At a college football game, a reporter asked the winning coach, "Is it true that you carry a chaplain along to pray for your team?"

"Certainly," the coach nodded.

"Could I interview him?"

"Of course. Which one do you want, our offensive or defensive chaplain?"

Strike when the iron is hot—not when the head is hot.

Minister to wayward church member: "I understand you played racquetball instead of going to church last Sunday."

"That's a lie, and I have the fish to prove it!"

Wrestling is a sport that gets a hold on you.

Mental health is a big issue today; people go crazy in pursuit of it.

The college athlete was so dumb that he thought Shirley Temple was a synagogue.

Minor operation: one performed on somebody else.

Good News! A college athlete has just completed the first successful hernia transplant!

Did you read about that fellow who was sued by the government for operating a monopoly—five ski lodges and a hospital?

A bunch of high school athletes were caught at night in a lumberyard.

They were looking for the draft board.

Maybe they call it "take-home pay" because there is no other place you can afford to go with it.

A famous ball player, when asked of his career, stated: "It's not the ups and downs of life that bother the average player. It's the jerks."

A college athlete solved the parking problem on campus.

He bought a parked car.

All right, sports. Hang tough. Keep a stiff upper lip. Bow your neck. Put your best foot forward. Keep your eye on the ball and your head down. Pace yourself. Give it all you got. Never look over your shoulder. Key in on the ball. Come out fighting. Win one for the Gipper.

And you'll be in one crazy, twisted position!